Mama TESTS Positive

Written by Jenni Jam
Illustrated by Gela Maravilla
Edited by Hayley Merchant

When people all around the world started to get sick, Mama told her Little One about the **pandemic**.

One day Mama got a text
to pick up Little One right away.
"I'm feeling unwell, please come soon"
the dayhome's text did say.

So Mama left her work behind,
and went to get her kid.
Driving home she said to him
**"Let's hope that it's
not COVID!"**

Day Home:
Mom...

But, alas, a few days later
another fateful text did chime.
"I'm shocked! I tested positive."
is what it said this time.

Mama sure felt shocked as well.
Did they have COVID too?
To find the answer, getting tested
is what they had to do.

All three tests were negative but quarantine was needed. Stay at home for **14 days** was the direction they proceeded.

It was around day fourteen that Mama felt unwell, and just a few days later she had **lost her sense of smell.**

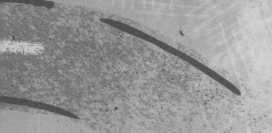

So off again Mama went to do another test.
She wasn't feeling confident, but she was **hoping for the best.**

Another text - the results were in.
It was Mama's turn to fight.
She had gotten COVID and isolation was in sight.

Papa and Little One tested too,
but came back negative.
So Mama packed herself a bag,
in the basement she would live.

Mama had to wear a mask
and wash her hands a lot.
**She tried her best to
stay positive** but it was
harder than she thought.

Headaches and fatigue
were the symptoms Mama had.
But among the pain and yawns
she found reasons to be glad.

Mama welcomed her time alone –
A break from cooking and cleaning!

hold 2.3.4

exhale

inhale 2.3.4

2.3.4

hold 2.3.4

Instead, she filled her time
doing things that brought
her **joy** and **meaning.**

She practiced new ways of breathing
through yoga and meditation
and later, in the afternoons,
she took naps for relaxation.

Mama channeled her creativity
into drawing and colouring art.
The first was a crown and mask-wearing cat
with a message straight from the heart.

Pineapples were drawn as well, of course
'Cause Mama's in love with those.
One dancing, and one doing yoga,
cross-legged in easy pose.

Papa fed Mama well every day
with greens and avocados on toast.
But his yummy smoothies, with fruits and nut butter
were what Mama loved the most!

Taking over a mama's role
was really quite the plateful.
For all of the care that Papa gave,
Mama felt forever grateful.

After two weeks, Mama's symptoms subsided
and she hoped that that was all...
She did not know it then that she
would be in it for the **long haul!**

Mama thought about her family's future
and could tell that it was bright.
She could feel something new inside
but had to make sure **she was right...**

So Mama went to her doctor
for a different kind of test, but this
time testing positive would simply
be the best.

Staying happy, healthy, and strong,
is what Mama knew she had to do...
For since she tested **positive**
she was eating now for two!

Mama shared the happy news
and could not stop from grinning.
It is true what they say:
In every end is a **new beginning.**

Dedicated to all the other Mamas out there who tested *positive after* testing *positive.*

Jenni Jam a.k.a Jennifer Campbell is a Canadian author, early childhood educator and mother of two beautiful boys. She tested positive for COVID-19 in early 2021 and battled her symptoms for over three months.

During isolation Jenni was inspired to share her unique story in an uplifting and permanent way, hence the idea to write Mama Tests Positive was born. Look for more books by Jenni Jam soon!

Did you know the pineapple drawings in this book were drawn by Jenni while she had COVID? Her pineapple obsession has been long-running and continues to this day!

Follow me 🄾 @jen.jenni.jam

Angelica Cabrera a.k.a. Gela Maravilla is a Graphic Designer and Illustrator based in Edmonton, AB, originally from Veracruz, Mexico.

Gela has over a decade of studio and freelance experience that spans from Mexico to Canada, most recently bringing her talents to the literary world with Mama Tests Positive.

This project has been an inspiring outlet for Gela's creative freedom as an illustrator, serving as a bright light amid these dim pandemic years.

You can find Gela's artwork and graphic design portfolio on Instagram as @gelamaravillailustration and @gelopolisdesign!

Manufactured by Amazon.ca
Bolton, ON